THE HAIRY BAKERS

HEALTHY DOGGIE SNACKS FOR YOU TO MAKE AT HOME

By Mungo & Tilly Trotter

Mungo Trotter

THE PAWLOG

Welcome to our cook book,

This book aims to provide you with ideas to keep you happy and healthy. All the recipes are very simple and use a wide variety of ingredients that my mummy [Tilly] and I love, but each one has very few ingredients – which means they are quick and easy to prepare. Some are for you to take on a walk where your owner may want to show their appreciation of how good you are. Or maybe to share with other canine friends on a walk, this will make you more popular with other doggie friends in the neighbourhood. Others are for bed time snacks, or when your owners think you look particularly adorable. (my mummy and I always do) They also have a wide variety of nutrients which are very good for us.

PEAMUTT BUTTER TREATS

Perfect for "good dog" treats take them in a bag on a walk or as a bed time treat.
I use 2cm. ¾" size cutters for walk snacks and larger ones for bed time.

INGREDIENTS

280g 2 cups plain / All purpose flour
120g ½ cup peanut butter
2 eggs
50 ml scant ¼ cup water

METHOD

1. Turn oven to 180°C 350°F gas 4
2. Mix the ingredients together until combined
3. Add water until it becomes wet enough to form a dough.
4. Roll out with a rolling pin and cut small discs
5. Place on a baking / cooking sheet
6. Bake for 20 minutes

Portia and Sophie

Rhum

Daisy

Bailey, Piper and Bella

SWEET POTATO WEDGES WITH CINNAMON AND TURMERIC

These provide us with some fresh vegetables, I don't know about you but we don't like raw vegetables! Coconut oil is good for our skin, digestive and immune systems. Adding turmeric, which is anti inflammatory, helps stiff joints and arthritis and cinnamon helps prevent diabetes and yeast infections. These are also delicious for humans!

INGREDIENTS

2 sweet potatoes (one for you and one for your owner!) (or two for you!)
Tblsp of coconut oil
½ tsp cinnamon
½ tsp turmeric

METHOD

1 Turn the oven to 200°C 400°F gas 6
2 Cut the sweet potatoes into wedges
3 Toss them in a bowl with the oil and spices
4 Place in a roasting tin and cook in the oven for 30 minutes until brown

Monty

Guiness Eagle

Chess

Tammy

APPLE AND CARROT "BITES"

We don't like raw carrots or apples but these crunchy treats are delicious, try mixing in a little cinnamon as well.

INGREDIENTS

120g 1 cup wholemeal / whole-wheat flour
120g 1 cup grated carrots
120g 1cup grated apple
1 egg

METHOD

1 Turn the oven to 180°C 350°F gas 4
2 Mix all the ingredients together and roll into about 10 small balls 3 Place on a baking / cookie sheet
4 Bake in the oven until crisp and firm about 30 minutes

Bertie

Indi, Holly, Corton and Aloxe

TUNA AND OATMEAL BAKE

This can also be made with the trimmings from fresh fish including the skin, in which case you may need a little more oil.

INGREDIENTS

150g 1 cup rolled / flaked oats
120g 1 cup cornflour / cornstarch
40g ⅓ cup rye flour
2 tbsp mixed fresh herbs, mint, parsley, dill or whatever you have
1 can tuna (or salmon) in oil
3 tblsp extra-virgin olive oil
1 egg
50 ml scant ¼ cup water

METHOD

1. Preheat the oven to 180°C 350°F. Gas 4
2. Mix together the oats, cornflour, rye flour with the herbs in a large bowl
3. Using a wooden spoon mash the tuna, oil, water and egg until Well mixed together
4. Make a well in the centre of the oat mixture and stir in the tuna mixture, add more water if the mixture seems too dry
5. Line a baking tray with greaseproof paper
6. Roll out the mixture on a lightly floured surface (use rye flour) and cut out your chosen shapes using a cutter heart shapes are nice! But your hound will not mind!
7. Bake for 25 minutes, then leave to cool completely on a wire rack

Milly

Pippi

UNCLE JAYK'S CHICKEN LIVER AND BACON TREATS

This recipe is from my daddy's owner, in Argyll

INGREDIENTS

125g 4oz streaky bacon rashers cut into thick strips
250g 8oz chicken livers (pigs will do as well) cut up roughly
250g 8oz plain or wholemeal flour
125g 4ozs of fine polenta / cornmeal
150ml ⅔ cup water

GLAZE

60g 2oz of tomato ketchup
1 large egg white
(Whisk the egg white and ketchup together to make a thick glaze, and set aside)

METHOD

1 Preheat oven to 125°C 260°F Gas3
2 Cook the bacon in large pan over medium-high heat until fairly crisp. Remove from the pan and set aside
3 Add the chicken livers, to the pan and cook stirring occasionally for 5 minutes or so, set pan aside to cool slightly
4 Put cooked bacon into a food processor and spin to form a coarse texture, then add the cooked chicken livers and process again to form a paste
5 Add the polenta and flour to form a coarse pâté mixture
6 Finally pour the water into the frying pan and heat gently and scrape up the juices, pour into the food processor, and spin to form a soft dough
7 Take the dough from the processor and knead it to form a smooth ball. Roll it out to about 1cm ⅜". Then use a small cutter to cut about 35 treats, depending on the size or shape of your cutter! And place on a baking sheet
7 Bake for 1 ½ hours
8 Take biscuits out of the oven and brush with the tomato ketchup glaze before baking for another 20 minutes
Allow to cool on a rack and store in an airtight container

Doramina Wemyss

Brodie

(CHOCK)LICK LIVER MORSELS

We have tried this with all livers, and when done it looks like chocolate!
[Which we aren't allowed but it's nice to think its chocolate]
Otherwise its biltong for dogs.

INGREDIENTS AND METHOD

1 Simply take 450g 1lb of ox / beef liver,
2 Preheat the oven to 180°C 350°F
3 Line a baking tray with parchment
4 Cut the liver into 1 cm ½" strips, place on the baking sheet and bake for around 2 hours. Make sure they are dry on the bottom

These will keep in the fridge in an airtight tin for 2 weeks, or will freeze for up to 4 months

It is always important to plan your route before setting out on a walk. Doggie snacks are part of the essential kit.

Oatie and Dougal

CHEESE & GARLIC DOG BISCUITS FROM DOGGIE PADDLES

These are one of our favourites and garlic in small quantities is good for us it helps with our digestive tract and also helps keep fleas and ticks away, what's not to like!

INGREDIENTS

100g 1 ½ cups wholemeal SR flour
120g 1 ¼ cups grated cheddar type cheese
115g 4oz butter
1 clove garlic, crushed
2fl oz ¼ cup milk

METHOD

1. Pre-heat oven to 190°C 350°F gas 5 and line baking / cookie sheets with greaseproof paper
2. Cream the cheese with the butter, add the garlic, salt and flour
3. Add enough milk to form a ball
4. Roll out on a floured surface and cut into shapes and place on the sheets
5. Bake for 15 mins
6. Leave to cool and serve to good doggies

Fergus and Freddie

Yipee...
Hairy Baker snacks!

BREATH FRESHENERS

We have never managed to brush our teeth, but these lovely biscuits with the fresh herbs really help, the activated charcoal (available on line) also helps reduce toxicity in our bodies.

INGREDIENTS

250g 2 cups brown rice flour
1 tblsp activated charcoal
3 tblsp peanut oil
1 egg
Tblsp ½ cup chopped fresh mint
Tblsp ½ cup chopped fresh parsley
160ml ⅔ cup milk

METHOD

1. Preheat oven to 200°C 400°F gas 6
2. Lightly oil a baking / cookie sheet
3. Combine flour and charcoal, add all the other ingredients
4. Drop teaspoonfuls onto the oiled sheet, about 2cm / 1" apart
5. Bake for 15-20 minutes

Store in airtight container in the refrigerator

Hardy

Harvey and Jarvis

DELIVERICIOUS SQUARES

Don't be alarmed by the quantity of garlic as I said before, it's good for us and these are special occasion treats

INGREDIENTS

450g 1 lb. Ox / beef liver
120g 1 cup whole wheat / wheat meal flour
140g 1 cup polenta / cornmeal
14 cloves garlic
2 eggs

METHOD

1. Turn oven to 180°C 350°F gas 4
2. Puree liver and garlic in food processor, add eggs, whole wheat flour and polenta.
3. Line a baking / cookie sheet with cling film / wrap and pour the mixture onto it.
4. Bake in the oven for 20 minutes, flipping over halfway through baking.
5. Cut into desired sized squares. You can put ½ of this recipe in a tupperware and keep in the fridge. The other half you can freeze… these freeze well.

Labradoodle puppies

Baxter

Boo and Yogie

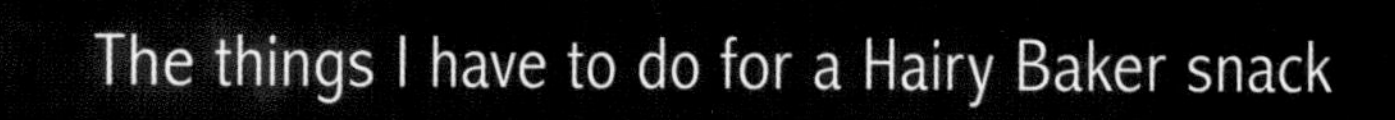

Molly

BANANA BARKOTTI'S

Bananas are high in potassium – good for our muscle structure and also have fibre which keeps us "regular". Very delicious for owners too – but don't tell them!

INGREDIENTS

500g 5 cups plain / all purpose flour
50g ¼ cup peanuts chopped
½ tsp baking powder
1 egg
50 ml ¼ cup vegetable oil
4 bananas, pureed
2 tsp vanilla essence
water

METHOD

1 Preheat oven to 170°C 325°F. Gas 3
2 Place dry ingredients in large bowl, make a well in the centre.
3 Blend egg, oil and banana together. and pour into the well
4 Mix together, adding water, one teaspoon at a time as needed.
5 Knead by hand on the table until mixed thoroughly.
6 Form into 2 logs approximately 5cm 2 ½" high, flatten so that the log will be elliptical.
7 Place on baking / cooking sheets lined with greaseproof and bake for 30 minutes. Remove and cool for 10 minutes, then cut in biscotti size pieces 1cm ½" approx.
8 Return to the oven and cook for another 20 minutes until golden brown cool on a rack and store in an air tight container

My dad – Boris

Truffles

Me – one day old

Me – four weeks old (big feet!)

Me – six weeks old

Me – one year old

THE TAIL END

NOTES FOR OWNERS

Please don't give us chocolate, raisins or grapes, they are not good for us and you will notice there is no salt or sugar in any of my recipes, there is enough naturally occurring in the ingredients.

These are our favourite recipes but please also remember that these are only meant as treats or rewards and do not take the place of our proper food!

Wags to:-

- Mistress the renowned doggy photographer and for the sitting fees. www.carolinetrotter.co.uk Contact her if you would like your portrait doing
- My mummy (Tilly) for having me
- And Master for helping me with the recipes

More books available from www.christophertrotter.co.uk

The End